READ, REFLECT, PRAY:
A LUTHERAN PRAYER BOOK

Read, Reflect, Pray:

A Lutheran Prayer Book

Compiled by

Pastor Chris Halverson

Read, Reflect, Pray: A Lutheran Prayer Book
Copyright © 2013, Christopher Lee Halverson
All rights reserved
First Printing: November 2013
Second Printing: June 2014

Scripture quotations are from New Revised Standard Version Bible, copyright © 1989 National Council of the Churches of Christ in the United States of America. Used by permission. All rights reserved.

The compiler gratefully acknowledges permission to reproduce the following copyrighted material:

Bonhoeffer, Dietrich.
Ethics by Dietrich Bonhoeffer, translated from the German by Neville Horton. Copyright © 1955 by SCM Press Ltd. Copyright © 1955 by Macmillan Publishing Company. All rights reserved. Reprinted with the permission of Scribner Publishing Group.
Letters and Papers from Prison by Dietrich Bonhoeffer, translated from the German by R.H. Fuller, Frank Clark , et al. Copyright © 1953, 1967, 1971 by SCM Press Ltd. All rights reserved. Reprinted with the permission of Scribner Publishing Group.
A Testament to Freedom: The Essential Writings of Dietrich Bonhoeffer by Geffrey B. Kelly and F. Burton Nelson (Eds.) Copyright © 1991 by Geffrey B. Kelly and F. Burton Nelson. All rights reserved. Reprinted with permission of HarperCollins Publishers.
Life Together by Deitrich Bonhoeffer, and translated by John Doberstein. English translation copyright © 1954 by Harper & Brothers, copyright renewed 1982 by Helen S. Doberstein. All rights reserved. Reprinted with permission of HarperCollins Publisher.

Doberstein, John W.
Minister's Prayer Book: An Order of Prayers and Readings.

Philadelphia, PA: Fortress Press, 1986. All rights reserved. Reprinted with the permission of Augsburg Fortress Press.
A Lutheran Prayer Book. Philadelphia, PA: Muhlenberg Press, 1960. All rights reserved. Reprinted with the permission of Augsburg Fortress Press.

Forde, Gerhard O. *Justification by Faith – A Matter of Death and Life.* Mifflintown, PA: Sigler Press, 1990. All rights reserved. Reprinted with the permission of Marianna Forde.

Forman, Mary. *Praying with the Desert Mothers.* Collegeville, MN: Liturgical Press, 2005. All rights reserved. Reprinted with the permission of Liturgical Press.

Krych, Margret A. *The Ministry of Children's Education: Foundations, Contexts, and Practices.* Minneapolis, MN: Augsburg Fortress, 2004. All rights reserved. Reprinted with the permission of Augsburg Fortress Press.

Lathrop, Gordon W.
The Pastor: A Spirituality. Minneapolis, MN: Fortress Press, 2006. All rights reserved. Reprinted with the permission of Augsburg Fortress Press.
Central Things. Minneapolis, MN: Augsburg Fortress, 2005. All rights reserved. Reprinted with the permission of Augsburg Fortress Press.
Luther, Martin. *Luther's Small Catechism, Study Edition: With Evangelical Lutheran Worship Texts.* Trans. Timothy Wengert. Minneapolis, MN: Augsburg Fortress, 2008. All rights reserved. Reprinted with the permission of Augsburg Fortress Press.

Ramshaw, Gail. *A Three-Year Banquest: The Lectionary for the Assembly* Minneapolis, MN: Augsburg Fortress, 2004. All rights reserved. Reprinted with the permission of Augsburg Fortress Press.

Thurman, Howard. *Jesus and the Disinherited*. Boston, MA: Beacon Press, 1976. All rights reserved. Reprinted with permission of Beacon Press, Boston.

Baptism, Eucharist, Ministry. Geneva: World Council of Churches, 1983.

Collects and Prayers: For Use in Church, Philadelphia, PA: The Board of Publications of the United Lutheran Church in America, 1935. All rights reserved. Reprinted with the permission of Augsburg Fortress Press.

Evangelical Lutheran Worship. Minneapolis, MN: Augsburg Fortress, 2006. All rights reserved. Reprinted with the permission of Augsburg Fortress Press.

The Book of Common Prayer. New York, New York: Church Publishing Incorporated, 2007. All rights reserved. Reprinted with permission of Church Publishing.

The Lutheran Hymnary. Minneapolis, MN: Augsburg Publishing House, 1913. All rights reserved. Reprinted with the permission of Augsburg Fortress Press.

Table of Contents

Preface 9

Acknowledgements 10

Introduction 11

How to use this prayer book 13

Dedication 15

The Morning Blessing 16

Sunday: Gathering in Community 17
    Read: 18
        Scripture about Gathering in Community: 18
        Scripture from the Torah: 18
        Meditations to Reflect upon 19
    Reflect: The First Three Commandments 26
    Pray: 28
        An invitation to prayer: 28
        A Prayer of Augustine of Hippo: 28
        Intercessions: 28
        Benediction: 30

Monday: Confession and forgiveness 31
    Read: 32
        Scripture about Confession and Forgiveness: 32
        Scripture from the Prophets: 32
        Meditations to Reflect upon 33
    Reflect: How People are to be Taught to Confess 39
    Pray: 40
        An invitation to prayer: 40
        A prayer attributed to Francis of Assisi: 40
        Intercessions: 41
        Benediction: 42

Tuesday: Baptism 43
    Read: 44
        Scripture about Baptism: 44
        Scripture from the Writings: 44
        Meditations to Reflect upon 45
    Reflect: The Sacrament of Holy Baptism 50
    Pray: 52

    An invitation to prayer: 52
    A prayer of Catherine of Siena: 53
    Intercessions: 53
    Benediction: 54

Wednesday: The Word 55
Read: 56
    Scripture about the Word: 56
    Scripture from Jesus' life: 56
    Meditations to Reflect upon 57
Reflect: The Creed 64
Pray: 67
    An invitation to prayer: 67
    A prayer of Julian of Norwich: 67
    Intercessions: 68
    Benediction: 69

Thursday: Thanksgiving 70
Read: 71
    Scripture about Thanksgiving: 71
    Scripture from Jesus' death: 71
    Meditations to Reflect upon: 72
Reflect: The Lord's Prayer 78
Pray: 83
    An invitation to prayer: 83
    A prayer of Martin Luther: 83
    Intercessions: 83
    Benediction: 85

Friday: The Meal 87
Read: 88
    Scripture about The Meal: 88
    Scripture from Jesus' Resurrection: 88
    Meditations to Reflect upon 89
Reflect: The Sacrament of the Altar 94
Pray: 96
    An invitation to prayer: 96
    A prayer of Mother Teresa of Calcutta: 96
    Intercessions: 96
    Benediction: 97

Saturday: The Sending 99
Read: 100

    Scripture about the Sending:..100
    Scripture from the Christian Letters:..100
    Meditations to Reflect upon..101
Reflect: The 4th through 10th commandments.................................107
Pray:..110
    An invitation to prayer:..110
    A Prayer of St. Patrick:...110
    Intercessions:..111
    Benediction:..112
The Evening Blessing: 113

Preface

I'm not exactly sure how this book started. Maybe it started with my struggle to find good resources for prayer, maybe it was coming into contact with Lathrop's *The Pastor* and Doberstein's *Minister's Prayer Book*, maybe it was an assignment in seminary to update Doberstein's book, maybe it was the spiritual blossoming I experienced as a Field Education Student and Intern at Tabernacle Lutheran in Philadelphia and St. John's Pimlico in Baltimore. I don't know.

But I do know that it came to a head when Hurricane Sandy hit. I was without power and my gas tank was empty, so, when I wasn't out checking in on parishioners, I had some free time. By candle and flashlight I started to compile prayer resources I'd used, think how they could all be fit into one book, and how the book could be organized in a useful way.

And out of that exercise produced by cabin fever and being disconnected from the internet, comes this book, *Read, Reflect, Pray*. I hope it aids you in your prayer life.

Acknowledgements

You never know how many people are going to be involved in something until you do it.

I wish to thank the following people for helping make this book a reality:

Fred Becker and Kelly Lundahl for their organizational and spatial eyes.

Kristin Walker for the beautiful new versions of Luther's Rose.

The 2013 Region 7 Leadership Guild, my congregation, St. Stephen Lutheran, and my mother, Valerie Halverson, for being my guinea pigs.

Clint Schnekloth, who pointed out the original edition of this book was breaking copyright.

Marianna Forde for giving permission to use her late husband's work—she's writing his biography so keep watch!

Anita Manbodh of Church Press, Christine J. Lee of Simon & Schuster Press, Colleen Haider of Liturgical Press, Karen Sigler of Sigler Press, Michael Moore of Augsburg Fortress Press, Rebecca Goldsmith of SCM Press, Ryan Mita of Beacon Press, and Trysha Le of HarperCollins Press, who all helped me navigate the publishing world.

Introduction

Greetings fellow prayers. As you can see this prayer book is built on three pillars; the *Ordo* of the Service of Holy Communion, Luther's Small Catechism, and portions of scripture from both the Earlier and Later Testaments.

I constructed this prayer book (specifically the daily themes) out of the first pillar — the *Ordo* — because of my belief that we do the things we do in worship, not for worship alone, but also in order to practice what we are to be in the world.

For example, we confess and find forgiveness not only because we are humans desperately in need of a word of grace, but also because we ought to confess and forgive on a regular basis. These ritual acts are also human acts, filled with importance for the world around us, not to mention for our own sanity and sanctity. Focusing our week on seven key elements of the liturgy — Gathering in Community, Confession and Forgiveness, Remembrance of Baptism, the Word, Giving Thanks, the Meal, and Sending should spread out our awareness of these gifts for our sake and the sake of those we interact with during the week — all for the glory of God through Jesus Christ.

Luther's Small Catechism has been a foundation for generations of Christians — it grounds us in the commands of Moses and the Prayer of Jesus, it reminds us of the common confession and the sacraments.

Some of the connections I made between the *Ordo* and the Catechism are obvious — the question "What should I confess?" clearly resonates with the daily theme of

Confession and Forgiveness. Other connections are less obvious—for example, I connected the seven last commandments to the daily theme of Sending in order to remind us that we are sent out to interact with fellow humans in a way that matches up to the ethics espoused in those commandments. Likewise, I connected the first three commandments to Gathering in Community because we gather as a community centered on God (and on the Sabbath), which is the focus of the first three commandments. As a final explanation, the creed is linked to the daily theme of the Word because the creed is a very brief summary of scripture—a mini-bible if you will. You will also notice Luther's explanation of a petition of the Lord's Prayer, in prayer form, begins each Intersession section.

    Finally, this prayer book's third pillar is scripture. As a Lutheran *Sola Scriptura* is a watchword of the faith that should not be ignored in one's prayer life.

    Not every book of the Bible shows up, but I tried to offer a fairly wide sampling—painting the story of God's interaction with us with a broad brush—yet also with an obvious bias to scriptures describing Jesus' life, death, and resurrection. In addition to pointing out a wider sampling of scripture, I also supplement the first pillar of the *Ordo* by pointing to biblical foundations and examples of the seven themes.

How to use this prayer book

Read, Reflect, Pray is a riff of Luther's prayer practice of *meditatio, tentatio, oratio*. The practice I recommend is beginning and ending the day with Luther's morning and evening prayer, and at some point in between those two prayers to pray through the particular day you are on (for example on Monday you pray through the section titled "Monday: Confession and Forgiveness).

This process begins with grounding yourself in scripture—read one scripture about the daily theme and one scripture from the section of the bible of the day (for example, on Monday you read "Scripture about Confession and Forgiveness" and "Scripture from the Prophets").

Additionally, in the sections entitled "Meditations to Reflect upon," there are readings about the daily theme with which to more fully center yourself.

Then reflect with Luther on that daily theme *via* a section of his catechism (allow a little time to reflect when you read this).

From there, give some time to think about the question provided about the day's theme (for example on Monday reflect on the question "What sin that you have committed in the last week most grieves you? Pray about it—talk it through with a sibling in the faith.").

As a transition from reflection to prayer recite (or if you can carry a tune sing it out) the invitation to prayer and begin praying an intercession or two, and from there launch off on your own prayers, letting the readings and your reflections lead you.

Don't forget to pray for the church, the world, and all those in need.

Then, when you've finished with your prayers give your prayer a sense of finality with a benediction. Finally, as Luther writes "go to your work (or play) joyfully."

Dedication

Finally, I would like to dedicate this book to Professor Timothy Wengert, whose Lutheran Spirituality class not only shaped my "spiritual" sensibilities, but also brought me into contact with both Doberstein's *Minister's Prayer* Book as well as Lathrop's *The Pastor: A Spirituality*. Dr. Wengert has faithfully taught a generation of Pastors what Luther confessed and how we ourselves might confess our faith in Jesus Christ.
Thank you.

The Morning Blessing

In the morning, as soon as you get out of bed, you are to make the sign of the holy cross and say:

"God the Father, Son, and Holy Spirit watch over me. Amen."

Then, kneeling or standing, say the Apostles' Creed and the Lord's Prayer. If you wish, you may in addition recite this little prayer as well:

"I give thanks to you, heavenly Father, through Jesus Christ your dear Son, that you have protected me through the night from all harm and danger. I ask that you would also protect me today from sin and all evil, so that my life and actions may please you. Into your hands I commend myself: my body, my soul, and all that is mine. Let your holy angels be with me, so that the wicked foe have no power over me. Amen."

SUNDAY

Sunday: Gathering in Community

"For where two or three are gathered in my name, I am there among them." (Matthew 18:20)

Read:

Scripture about Gathering in Community:

Acts 2:1-13
Exodus 20:8-11
Revelation 7:9
Hebrews 10:24-25
Isaiah 48: 14

Scripture from the Torah:

Genesis 1:1-2:3
Genesis 2:4-25
Genesis 12:1-3
Genesis 50:15-21
Exodus 3:1-14
Exodus 20:1-17
Leviticus 19:1-2
Numbers 6:22-27
Deuteronomy 8:7-10
Deuteronomy 32:48-52

Meditations to Reflect upon

The Center of Gathering

"More Lutheran Christians argue that the things we do in the Christian assembly should primarily be the things that make it possible to believe in God at all." — Lathrop

"The essentials for Christian worship are an open and participating community gathered on the Lord's Day in song and prayer around the scriptures read and preached, around the baptismal washing, enacted or remembered, around the holy supper, and around the sending to a needy world." — Lathrop

Christianity and Power

"Many and varied are the interpretations dealing with the teachings and the life of Jesus of Nazareth. But few of these interpretations deal with what the teachings and the life of Jesus have to say to those who stand, at a moment in human history, with their backs against the wall.

To those who need profound succor and strength to enable them to live in the present with dignity and creativity, Christianity often has been sterile and of little avail. The conventional Christian world is muffled, confused, and vague. Too often the price exacted by society for security and respectability is that the Christian movement in its formal expression must be on the side of the strong against the weak. This is a matter of tremendous significance, for it reveals to what extent a religion that was born of a people acquainted with persecution and suffering has become the cornerstone of a civilization and of nations whose very position in modern life has too often been secured by a ruthless use of power applied to weak and defenseless peoples." — Thurman

"The elimination of the weak is the death of the community." — Bonhoeffer

"We drank our coffee in silence. After the service had been removed, he said to me, "What are you doing over here? I know that the newspapers say about a pilgrimage of friendship and the rest, but that is not my question. What are you doing over here? This is what I mean.

More than three hundred years ago your forefathers were taken from the western coast of Africa as slaves. The people who dealt in the slave traffic were Christians. One of your famous Christian hymn writers, Sir John Newton, made his money from the sale of slaves to the New World. He is the man who wrote 'How Sweet the Name of Jesus Sounds' and 'Amazing Grace' — there may be others, but these are the one ones I know. The name of one of the famous British slave vessels was 'Jesus.'

The men who bought the slaves were Christians. Christian ministers, quoting the Christian apostle Paul, gave the sanction of religion to the system of slavery. Some seventy years or more ago you were freed by a man who was not a professing Christian, but was rather the spearhead of certain political, social, and economic forces, the significance of which he himself did not understand.

During all the period since then you have lived in a Christian nation in which you are segregated, lynched, and burned. Even in the church, I understand, there is segregation. One of my students who went to your country sent me a clipping telling about a Christian church in which the regular Sunday worship was interrupted so that many could join a mob against one of your fellows. When he had been caught and done to death, they came back to resume their worship of their Christian God.

I am a Hindu. I do not understand. Here you are in my country, standing deep within the Christian faith and tradition. I do not wish to seem rude to you. But, sir, I think you are a traitor to all the darker people of the earth. I am wondering what you, an intelligent man, can say in defense of your position." — Thurman

Jesus' people

"It is impossible for Jesus to be understood outside of the sense of community which Israel held with God." — Thurman

Diverse community

"The first step toward love is a common sharing of a sense of mutual worth and value. This cannot be discovered in a vacuum or in a series of artificial or hypothetical relationships. It has to be in a real situation, natural, free.

The experience of the common worship of God is such a moment. It is in this connection that American Christianity has betrayed the religion of Jesus almost beyond redemption. Churches have been established for the underprivileged, for the weak, for the poor, on the theory that they prefer to be among themselves. Churches have been established for the Chinese, the Japanese, the Korean, the Mexican, the Filipino, the Italian, and the Negro, with the same theory in mind. The result is that in the one place in which normal, free contacts might be more naturally established—in which the relations of the individual to his God should take priority over conditions of class, race, power, status, wealth, or the like—this place is one of the chief instruments for guaranteeing barriers." —Thurman

"God does not want me to mold others into the image that seems good to me, that is, into my own image. Instead, in their freedom from me God made other people into God's own image. I can never know in advance how God's image should appear in others. That image always takes on a completely new and unique form whose origin is found solely in God's free and sovereign act of creation. To me that form may seem strange, even ungodly. But God creates every person in the image of God's Son, the Crucified, and this image, likewise, certainly looked strange and ungodly to me before I grasped it. Strong and weak, wise or foolish, talented or untalented, pious or less pious, the complete diversity of individuals in the community is no longer a reason to talk or judge and condemn, and therefore no longer a pretext for self-justification. Rather this diversity is a reason for rejoicing in one another and serving one another." — Bonhoeffer

The danger of a Wish-dream Community

"On innumerable occasions a whole Christian community has been shattered because it has lived on the basis of a wishful image. Certainly serious Christians who are put in a community for the first time will often bring with them a very definite image of what Christian communal life should be, and they will be anxious to realize it. But God's grace quickly frustrates all such dreams. A great disillusionment with others, with Christians in general, and, if we are fortunate, with ourselves, is bound to overwhelm us as surely as God desires to lead us to an understanding of genuine Christian community. By sheer grace God will not permit us to live in a dream world even for a few weeks and to abandon ourselves to those blissful experiences and exalted moods that sweep over us like a wave of rapture. For God is not a God of emotionalism, but the God of truth. Only the community which enters into the experience of this great disillusionment with all its unpleasant and evil appearances begins to be what it should be in God's sight, begins to grasp in faith the promise that is given to it." — Bonhoeffer

"Those who love their dream of a Christian community more than the Christian community itself become destroyers of that Christian community even though their personal intentions may be ever so honest, earnest, and sacrificial." — Bonhoeffer

"Whoever cannot be alone should beware of community. Whoever cannot stand being in community should beware of being alone." — Bonhoeffer

Listening in Community

"Just as our love for God begins with listening to God's Word, the beginning of love for other Christians is learning to listen to them. God's love for us is shown by the fact that God not only gives us God's Word, but also lends us God's ear. We do God's work for our brothers and sisters when we learn to listen to them. So often Christians, especially preachers, think that their only service is always to have to "offer" something when they are together with other people. They forget that listening can be a greater service than speaking. Many people seek a sympathetic ear and do not find it among Christians, because these Christians are talking even when they should be listening. But Christians who can no longer listen to one another will soon no longer be listening to God either; they will always be talking even in the presence of God." — Bonhoeffer

Christianity and Christ today?

"What is bothering me incessantly is the question what Christianity really is, or indeed who Christ really is, for us today. The time when people could be told everything by means of words, whether theological or pious, is over, and so is the time of inwardness and conscience — and that means the time of religion in general. We are moving toward a completely religionless time; people as they are now simply cannot be religious anymore. Even those who honestly describe themselves as "religious" do not in the least act up to it, and so they presumably mean something quite different by "religious." Our whole 1,900-year-old Christian preaching and theology rest on the "religious a priori" of humanity. "Christianity" has always been a form — perhaps the true form — of "religion." But if one day it becomes clear that this a priori does not exist at all, but was a historically conditioned and transient form of human self-expression, and if therefore people become radically religionless—and I think that is already more or less the case (else how is it, for example, that this war, in contrast to all previous ones, is not calling forth any "religious" reaction?)—what does that mean for "Christianity"?" — Bonhoeffer

Reflect: The First Three Commandments

The First Commandment:

You shall have no other gods.

What does this mean?

We are to fear, love, and trust God above all things.

The Second Commandment:

You shall not make wrongful use of the name of the Lord your God.

What does this mean?

We are to fear and love God, so that we do not curse, swear, practice magic, lie, or deceive using God's name, but instead use the very name in every time of need to call on, pray to, praise, and give thanks to God.

The Third Commandment:

Remember the Sabbath day, and keep it holy.

What does this mean?

We are to fear and love God, so that we do not despise preaching or God's word, but instead keep that word holy and gladly hear and learn it.

Questions:

Who do you most look forward to seeing at church?
Who do you least look forward to seeing at church?
Remember to pray for them both.

Pray:

An invitation to prayer:

Lord have mercy.

Christ have mercy.

Lord have mercy.

A Prayer of Augustine of Hippo:

O loving God, to turn away from you is to fall, to turn toward you is to rise, and to stand before you is to abide forever. Grant us, dear God, in all our duties your help; in all our uncertainties your guidance; in all our dangers your protection; and in all our sorrows your peace; through Jesus Christ our Lord. Amen.

Intercessions:

"Hallowed be your Name."

O God, whose name is holy in and of itself, we pray that it may also become holy in and among us.

Help us blessed Father, that your word may be taught clearly and purely, and that we, as your children, may live according to it; through Jesus Christ, your Son, our Lord. Amen.

God of grace, you have given us minds to know you,

hearts to love you, and voices to sing your praise. Fill us with your Spirit, that we may celebrate your glory and worship you in spirit and truth, through Jesus Christ, our Savior and Lord. Amen.

Gracious Father, we pray for your holy catholic church. Fill it with all truth and peace. Where it is corrupt, purify it; where it is in error, direct it; where in anything it is amiss, reform it; where it is right, strengthen it; where it is in need, provide for it; where it is divided, reunite it; for the sake of Jesus Christ, your Son, our Lord. Amen.

For all who fear God and believe in you, Lord Christ, that our divisions may cease, and that all may be one as you and the Father are one, we pray to you O Lord. Amen.

O God our King, by the resurrection of your Son Jesus Christ on the first day of the week, you conquered sin, put death to flight, and gave us the hope of everlasting life: Redeem all our days by this victory; forgive our sins, banish our fears, make us bold to praise you and to do your will; and steel us to wait for the consummation of your kingdom on the Last Great Day; through the same Jesus Christ our Lord. Amen.

Continue praying on your own.

Benediction:

"The Lord bless you and keep you; the Lord make his face to shine upon you, and be gracious to you; the Lord lift up his countenance upon you, and give you peace." (Numbers 6:24-26)

May the almighty and merciful God, Father, Son, and Holy Spirit, bless and keep us. Amen.

MONDAY
confession and forgiveness

Monday: Confession and forgiveness

"If we say we have no sin, we deceive ourselves, and the truth is not in us. If we confess our sins, God who is faithful and just will forgive us our sins and cleanse us from all unrighteousness."

(1 John 1:8-9)

Read:

Scripture about Confession and Forgiveness:

Psalm 103:2-5
John 20:22-23
Ephesians 2:4-5
Ephesians 3:16-17

Prov. 28:13
Psalm 32:5
Psalm 51:1-17

Scripture from the Prophets:

Isaiah 6:1-8
Isaiah 25:6-10
Isaiah 40:1-5
Isaiah 52:13-53:12
Jeremiah 1:4-10
Jeremiah 32:14-15
Ezekiel 1:4-28
Ezekiel 37:1-14

Ezekiel 43:1-5
Daniel 3:10-28
Hosea 6:6
Amos 2:6-8
Jonah 4:10-11
Malachi 3:1-4

Meditations to Reflect upon

We are Bound to Sin, and Cannot Free Ourselves

"We abuse, we betray, we are cruel. We destroy, we embitter, we falsify. We gossip, we hate, we insult...," says one of the classic confessions of the Day of Atonement, rightly continuing to fill out the whole alphabet with our continual communal wrongs. — Lathrop

It would make no sense for God to forgive sins if we weren't actually sinners." — Forde

"The question is not one of what is "left over" for our freedom after all the prior and more powerful forces have had their way. The question is rather one of what we have done with the freedom we have been given. The question has to do with the way things are, the actual state and commitment of the will in its alienation from God. The Confessional and Reformation point is not that we don't have wills, nor is it that these wills are somehow frustrated by a transcendent bully or puppeteer, but rather that we have sold ourselves into a slavery from which there is no escape. And we have done this quite willingly." — Forde

"If sparks could set fire to the ocean, then indeed your sins could defile the purity of God!" — Forman

Humility, Hatred, Love

"Jesus had to resent deeply the loss of Jewish national independence and the aggression of

Rome…Natural humiliation was hurting and burning. The balm for that burning humiliation was humility. For humility cannot be humiliated.

Thus he asked his people to learn from him, "For I am meek and lowly in heart; and ye shall find rest unto your souls. For my yoke is easy, and my burden is light," — Vladimir Simkhovitch

"Christianity has been almost sentimental in its effort to deal with hatred in human life. It has sought to get rid of hatred by preachments, by moralizing, by platitudinous judgments. It has hesitated to analyze the basis of hatred and to evaluate it in terms of its possible significance in the lives of the people possessed by it." — Thurman

"Jesus rejected hatred. It was not because he lacked the vitality or the strength. It was not because he lacked the incentive. Jesus rejected hatred because he saw that hatred meant death to the mind, death to the spirit, death to communion with his Father. He affirmed life; and hatred was the great denial. To him it was clear.

Thou must not make division./Thy mind, heart, soul and strength must ever search/To find the way by which the road/To all men's need of thee must go./This is the Highway of the Lord." — Thurman

"Each person meets the other where he is and there treats him as if he were where he ought to be. Here we emerge into an area where love operates, revealing a universal characteristic unbounded by special or limited circumstances.

How did Jesus define it? One day a woman was brought to Jesus. She had been caught in the act of adultery. The spokesman for the group who brought her said she was caught red-handed and that according to the law she should be stoned to death. "What is your judgment?" was their searching question. To them the woman was not a woman, or even a person, but an adulteress, stripped of her essential dignity and worth. Said Jesus: "He that is without sin among you, let him first cast a stone." After that, he implied, any person may throw. The quiet words exploded the situation, and in the piercing glare each man saw himself in his literal substance. In that moment each was not a judge or another's deeds, but of his own. In the same glare the adulteress saw herself merely as a woman involved in the meshes of a struggle with her own elemental passion.

Jesus, always the gentleman, did not look at the woman as she stood before him. Instead he looked on the ground, busied himself with his thoughts. What a moment, reaching beyond time into eternity!

Jesus waited. One by one the men crept away. The woman alone was left. Hearing no outcry, Jesus raised his eyes and beheld the woman. "Where are those thine accusers? Hath no man condemned thee?"

"No man, Lord."

"Neither do I condemn thee: go and sin no more."

This is how Jesus demonstrated reverence for personality. He met the woman where she was, and he treated her as if she were already where she now willed to be. In dealing with her he "believed" her into the fulfillment of her possibilities. He stirred her confidence into activity. He placed a crown over her head which for the rest of her life she would keep trying to grow tall enough to wear.

Free at last, free at last,/Thank God Almighty, I'm free at last." — Thurman

Love of Enemy

"In the face of the cross the disciples realize that they too were his enemies and that he had overcome them by his love. It is this that opens the disciples' eyes and enables them to see their enemy as a brother or sister. They know that they owe their very life to One who, though he was their enemy, accepted them, who made them his neighbors, and drew them into community with himself. The disciples can now perceive that even their enemies are the object of God's love, and that they stand like themselves beneath the cross of Christ." — Bonhoeffer

"He knew his past and that past, though forgiven, was not forgotten, for his remembrance of that past helped him not to sit in judgment of anyone else." — Forman

Confession and Community

"In confession there takes place a breakthrough to community. Sin want to be alone with people. It takes them away from the community. The more lonely people become, the more destructive the power of sin over them. The more deeply they become entangled in it, the more unholy is their loneliness. Sin wants to remain unknown. It shuns the light. In the darkness of what is left unsaid sin poisons the whole being of a person. This can happen in the midst of a pious community. In confession the light of the gospel breaks into the darkness and closed isolation of the heart. Sin must be brought into the light. What is unspoken is said openly and confessed. All that is secret and hidden comes to light. It is a hard struggle until the sin crosses one's lips in confession. But God breaks down gates of bronze and cuts through bars of iron. Since the confession of sin is made in the presence of another Christian, the last stronghold of self-justification is abandoned. The sinner surrenders, giving up all evil, giving the sinner's heart to God and finding the forgiveness of all one's sin in the community of Jesus Christ and other Christians." — Bonhoeffer

"What would happen in communities and families if they trusted one another with the need for support through a loathsome temptation, and the one in whom the care was confided was willing to carry the burden in discretion and confidentiality by fasting and praying for the one in need? What if communities fasted and prayed for the abused children, battered wives, and broken husbands, siblings, and relatives we know? What channels of God's grace might our faith communities become for our world!" — Forman

"What is sin for an individual is never virtue for an entire people or nation." — Bonhoeffer

✣

"To achieve means always to begin again anew." — Luther

✣

Repentance

"In the Reformation, confession and forgiveness were sometimes together called "repentance." Speaking of that repentance, Luther once wrote these remarkable lines:

Therefore baptism remains forever. Even though someone falls from it and sins, we always have access to it so that we may again subdue the old creature. But we need not have the water poured over us again. Even if we were immersed in water a hundred times, it would nevertheless not be more than one baptism, and the effect and significance would continue and remain. Repentance, therefore, is nothing else than a return and approach to baptism, to resume and practice what has earlier been begun but abandoned…thus we see what a great and excellent thing baptism is, which snatches us from the jaws of the devil and makes us God's own, overcomes and takes away sin and daily strengthens the new person, and always endures and remains until we pass out of this misery into eternal glory. Therefore, let all Christians regard their baptism as the daily garment that they are wearing all the time." — Lathrop

Reflect: How People are to be Taught to Confess

What is confession?

Confession consists of two parts. One is that we confess our sins. The other is that we receive the absolution, that is, forgiveness, from the pastor as from God himself and by no means doubt but firmly believe that our sins are thereby forgiven before God in heaven.

Which sins is a person to confess?

Before God one is to acknowledge the guilt for all sins, even those of which we are not aware, as we do in the Lord's Prayer. However, before the pastor we are to confess only those sins of which we have knowledge and which trouble us.

Which sins are these?

Here reflect on your place in life in light of the Ten Commandments: whether you are father, mother, son, daughter, master, mistress, servant; whether you have been disobedient, unfaithful, lazy, whether you have harmed anyone by word or deed; whether you have stolen, neglected, wasted, or injured anything.

Question:

What sin that you have committed in the last week most grieves you? Pray about it—talk it through with a sibling in the faith.

Pray:

An invitation to prayer:

Merciful God, I confess

That I have sinned in thought, word, and deed,

By what I have done and by what I have left undone.

I repent of all my sins

I repent of all my sins, known and unknown.

I am truly sorry, and I pray for forgiveness.

I firmly intend to amend my life,

And to seek help in mending what is broken.

I ask for strength to turn from sin

And to serve you in newness of life.

Through Jesus Christ.

Amen.

A prayer attributed to Francis of Assisi:

Lord, make us instruments of your peace. Where there is hatred, let us sow love; where there is injury, pardon; where there is discord, union; where there is doubt, faith; where there is despair, hope; where there is darkness, light; where there is sadness, joy.

Grant that we may not so much seek to be consoled as to console; to be understood as to understand; to be loved as to love. For it is in giving that we receive; it is in pardoning that we are pardoned; and it is in dying that we are born to eternal life. Amen.

Intercessions:

"Your kingdom come."

O God, everlasting Father, whose kingdom comes on its own without our prayer, we pray that it may come also to us.

To this end give to us your Holy Spirit, so that through the Holy Spirit's grace we may believe your holy word, and live godly lives here in time and hereafter in eternity. Amen.

✤

Gracious God, your Son called on you to forgive his enemies while he was suffering shame and death. Lead our enemies and us from prejudice to truth; deliver them and us from hatred, cruelty, and revenge; and in your good time enable us all to stand reconciled before you; through Jesus Christ, our Savior and Lord. Amen.

✤

Lord Christ, you came into the world as one of us, and suffered as we do. As we go through the trials of life, help us to realize that you are with us at all times and in all things; that we have no secrets from you; and that your loving grace enfolds us for eternity. In the security of your embrace we pray. Amen.

✤

Save us, O God, from the spirit which leads to strife, from the tempter which refuses to forgive and has no wish to forget; and from lack of faith in the power to change human hearts; through Jesus Christ our Lord. Amen.

✜

Continue praying on your own.

Benediction:

The Lord bless you and keep you.

The Lord make his face shine on you and be gracious to you.

The Lord look upon you with favor and give you peace.

Amen.

✜

The God of peace, who brought back from the dead our Lord Jesus, make you complete in everything good so that you may do God's will, and work among you that which is pleasing in God's sight, through Jesus Christ our Lord. Amen.

TUESDAY
baptism

Tuesday: Baptism

"Do you not know that all of us who have been baptized into Christ Jesus were baptized into his death? Therefore we have been buried with him by baptism into death, so that, just as Christ was raised from the dead by the glory of the Father, so we too might walk in newness of life. For if we have been united with him in a death like his, we will certainly be united with him in a resurrection like his."(Romans 6:3-5)

Read:

Scripture about Baptism:

Galatians 3:27-29	2 Corinthians 5:17
Acts 8:36-38	Psalm 51:2
1 Corinthians 3:23	Matthew 28:18-20
Isaiah 11:2	Titus 3:5
Mark 1:9-11	

Scripture from the Writings:

Job 2	Psalm 23	Proverbs 28:11-28
Job 3:1-10	Psalm 51	Ecclesiastes 1:1-11
Job 4:1-9	Psalm 82	Ecclesiastes 3:1-8
Job 8:1-6	Psalm 150	
Job 11:1-6	Proverbs 1:1-7	
Job 38:1-11	Proverbs 6:6-11	
Job 42:7	Proverbs 8:22-31	
Psalm 1		

Meditations to Reflect upon

Declared Children of God

"God does not seek the most perfect human being with whom to be united, but takes on human nature as it is. Jesus Christ is not the transfiguration of noble humanity but the Yes of God to real human beings, not the dispassionate Yes of a judge but (the) merciful Yes of a compassionate sufferer. In this Yes all the life and all the hope of the world are comprised. In the human Jesus Christ the whole of humanity has been judged; again this is not the uninvolved judgment of a judge, but the merciful judgment of one who has borne and suffered the fate of all humanity. Jesus is not *a* human being but *the* human being. What happens to him happens to human beings. It happens to all and therefore to us. The name of Jesus embraces in itself the whole of humanity and the whole of God." — Bonhoeffer

"When I was a youngster, this was drilled into me by my grandmother. The idea was given to her by a certain slave minister who, on occasion, held secret religious meetings with his fellow slaves. How everything in me quivered with the pulsing tremor of raw energy when, in her recital, she would come to the triumphant climax of the minister: "You — you are not niggers. You — you are not slaves. You are God's children." This established for them the ground of personal dignity, so that a profound sense of personal worth could absorb the fear reaction. This alone is not enough, but without it, nothing else is of value. The first task is to get the self immunized against the most radical results of the threat of violence. When this is accomplished, relaxation takes the place of the churning fear. The individual now feels that he counts, that he belongs. He senses the confirmation of his roots, and even death becomes a little thing." — Thurman

"Jesus recognized with authentic realism that anyone who permits another to determine the quality of his inner life gives into the hands of the other the keys to his destiny." — Thurman

"The solution which Jesus found for himself and for Israel, as they faced the hostility of the Greco-Roman world, becomes the word and the work of redemption for all the cast-down people in every generation and in every age. I mean this quite literally. I do not ignore the theological and metaphysical interpretation of the Christian doctrine of salvation. But the underprivileged everywhere have long since abandoned any hope that this type of salvation deals with the crucial issues by which their days are turned into despair without consolation. The basic fact is that Christianity as it was born in the mind of this Jewish teacher and thinker appears as a technique of survival for the oppressed. That it became, through the intervening years, a religion of the powerful and the dominant, used sometimes as an instrument of oppression, must not tempt us into believing that it was thus in the mind and life of Jesus. "In him was life; and the life was the light of men." Wherever his spirit appear, the oppressed gather fresh courage; for he announced the good news that fear, hypocrisy, and hatred, the three hounds of hell that track the trail of the disinherited, need have no dominion over them." — Thurman

"So when the question is put, "You don't mean to

say grace is irresistible do you?" I think it more consonant with the truth of the matter to answer, "Yes, I find it to be so, don't you?" Likewise, for old questions such as, "Do you mean to say once saved, always saved?" Again, perhaps the best answer would be "What's the matter with that? I would hope so, wouldn't you?" —Forde

✣

Baptismal Vocation

"Ministry of the laity, however, is not primarily about letting a lay person preach, but rather about lifting up the varieties of vocations the baptized people of God engage in all week long." —Cook Everist

"But do not let this accusation turn you to cynicism or immobility. Say it again: dear pastor, creep back to the water. These accusations are true, and they do cast the shadow of your own failure, sin, and death. But, united with Christ, your death is already there in that water and you have been forgiven and raised to new life. Hear that word spoken to you—by your neighbor, your friend, your spouse, this book, the next liturgy in which you participate. The Spirit of the Risen One blows in the Word and from the water as well, and that Spirit keeps forming you for living—not dying—together with us all." —Lathrop

"Martin Luther, in his own vocation as teacher and preacher, understood his need to be a lifelong student of the catechism, to read and recite and ponder the Lord's Prayer, the Creed, the Ten Commandments, and, above all, to know that he was baptized. Even thought he was a pastor and professor in the church, Luther thought he had to be always beginning again, learning with the newest newcomer, the youngest child, the surprises of God's grace. He recommended this same study to everyone else, in whatever vocation. Not least of all, he recommended it to pastors and preachers. His words at his own death—"I say we are all beggars"—thus had an echo in his life as a constant beginner." —Lathrop

✛

"In order to overcome their differences, believer Baptists and those who practice infant baptism should reconsider certain aspects of their practices. The first may seek to express more visibly the fact that children are placed under the protection of God's grace. The later must guard themselves against the practice of apparently indiscriminate baptism and take more seriously their responsibility for the nurture of baptized children to mature commitment to Christ." —Baptism Eucharist Ministry

✛

Baptism and Death

"Even our funerals hold something of the water: the body set near the font or under the great garment of baptism (the pall) or near the great candle, and baptismal texts spoken or sung as grounds for the promise of life in the midst of death." —Lathrop

"The cross is laid on every Christian. The first Christ-suffering which every person must experience is the call to abandon the attachments of this world. It is that dying of the old person which is the result of our encounter with Christ. As we embark upon discipleship we surrender ourselves to Christ in union with his death—we give over our lives to death. Thus it begins; the cross is not the terrible end to an otherwise God-fearing and happy life, but it meets us at the beginning of our communion with Christ. When Christ calls us, he bids us come and die. It may be a death like that of the first disciples who had to leave home and work to follow him, or it may be a death like Luther's, who had to leave the monastery and go out into the world. But it is the same death every time—death in Jesus Christ, the death of the old person at his call." — Bonhoeffer

"If we would bear the image of his glory, we must first bear the image of his shame. There is no other way to recover the image we lost through the Fall." — Bonhoeffer

✣

"The two things of baptism—the name and the bath, side-by-side, or the water and the teaching—also press us toward a third: toward community with each other. That is, water and the name bringing us toward reminding each other of these things, toward communally bearing witness to the grace of God in the world. Baptism brings us to the assembly." — Lathrop

Reflect: The Sacrament of Holy Baptism

What is baptism?

Baptism is not simply plain water. Instead, it is water used according to God's command and connected with God's word.

What then is this word of God?

Where our Lord Christ says in Matthew 28, "Go therefore and make disciples of all nations, baptizing them in the name of the Father and of the Son and of the Holy Spirit."

What gifts or benefits does baptism grant?

It bring about forgiveness of sins, redeems from death and the devil, and gives eternal salvation to all who believe it, as the words and promise of God declare.

What are these words and promise of God?

Where our Lord Christ says in Mark 16, "The one who believes and is baptized will be saved, but the one who does not believe will be condemned."

How can water do such great things?

Clearly the water does not do it, but the word of God, which is with and alongside the water, and faith, which trusts this word of God in the water. For without the word of God the water is plain water and not a baptism, but with the word of God it is a baptism, that is, a grace-filled water of life and a "bath of the new birth in the Holy Spirit," as St. Paul says to Titus in chapter 3, "through the water of rebirth and renewal by the Holy Spirit. This Spirit he poured out on us richly through Jesus Christ our Savior, so that, having been justified by his grace, we might become heirs according to the hope of eternal life. The saying is sure."

What then is the significance of such a baptism with water?

It signifies that the old person in us with all sins and evil desires is to be drowned and die through daily sorrow for sin and through repentance, and on the other hand that daily a new person is to come forth and rise up to live before God in righteousness and purity forever.

Where is this written?

St. Paul says in Romans 6, "We have been buried with Christ by baptism into death, so that, just as Christ was raised from the dead by the glory of the Father, so we too might walk in newness of life."

Question:

　　Was there a time this week when you forgot you were a Child of God? A time you felt especially like a Child of God?

　　A time you forgot someone else was a Child of God? A time you remembered someone else was one?

Pray:

> An invitation to prayer:

(making the sign of the cross in remembrance of your baptism)

In the name of the Father

And of the Son,

And of the Holy Spirit.

Amen.

I am joined to Christ in the waters of baptism,

I am clothed with God's mercy and forgiveness.

For that I give you thanks.

Thank you for your Spirit that moved over the waters at creation, calling forth life in which you took delight.

Thank you for delivering Noah and his family through the waters of the flood.

Thank you for leading your people Israel from slavery into freedom.

Thank you for Jesus' baptism by John at the Jordon River and for his anointing with the Holy Spirit.

Thank you for claiming us through the water and your word as your daughters and sons, making us heirs of your promise and servants of all.

We praise you for the gift of water that sustains life, and

above all we praise you for the gift of new life in Jesus Christ.

Shower us with your Spirit, and renew our lives with your forgiveness, grace, and love.

To you be given honor and praise, through Jesus Christ our Lord, in the unity of the Holy Spirit, now and forever. Amen.

A prayer of Catherine of Siena:

Power of the eternal Father, help me. Wisdom of the Son, enlighten the eye of my understanding. Tender mercy of the Holy Spirit, unite my heart to yourself. Eternal God, restore health to the sick and life to the dead. Give us a voice, your own voice, to cry out to you for mercy for the world. You, light, give us light. You, wisdom, give us wisdom. You supreme strength, strengthen us. Amen.

Intercessions:

"Your will be done, on earth as in heaven."

O God, whose good and gracious will comes about without our prayer, we ask that it might also come about in and among us.

To this end, you break and hinder every evil scheme and will—such as the will of the devil, the world, and our flesh—for it would not allow us to hallow your name and would prevent the coming of your kingdom. Please strengthen us and keep us steadfast in your word and in faith until the end of our lives. May your gracious and good will be done. Amen.

✤

Lord God, in whose name I was baptized; you have called me by name and I belong to you. Grant that I may give myself to you, body, mind, and heart. Fill me now with a new loyalty and help me always to be true to you in faith and obedience until my life's end; through Jesus Christ our Lord. Amen.

✤

Almighty God, by our baptism into the death and resurrection of your Son, Jesus Christ, you turn us from the old life of sin. Grant that we who are reborn to new life in him may live in righteousness and holiness all our days, through Jesus Christ our Lord. Amen.

✤

Continue praying on your own.

Benediction:

"The LORD will preserve you from all evil and will keep your life. The LORD will watch over your going out and your coming in, from this time forth forevermore." (Psalm 121:7-8)

✤

The peace of God, which passes all understanding, keep your heart and mind in the knowledge and love of God, in Jesus Christ our Lord; and the blessing of Almighty God, Father, Son, and Holy Spirit, be among you and remain with you always. Amen.

WEDNESDAY
the word

Wednesday: The Word

"Hear the word of the LORD." (Jeremiah 2:4)

Read:

Scripture about the Word:

Isaiah 55:10-11
John 1:1-5, 14
Psalm 1:1-2

Colossians 3:16
1 Timothy 4:13
Nehemiah 8:5-6

Scripture from Jesus' life:

Luke 1:39-56
Mark 1:4-11
Matthew 4:1-11
Luke 6:17-49
John 13:34-35

Mark 9:2-8
John 6:1-15
John 10:1-18

Meditations to Reflect upon

Scripture

"The purpose of the texts is not for the assembly to imagine how things might have been in other times, but to encounter the biblical God, the God who comes now to this time with all biblical judgment and promise. So Luther wrote: "When you open the book containing the gospels and read or hear how Christ comes here or there, or how someone is brought to him, you should therein perceive the sermon or the gospel through which he is coming to you, or you are being brought to him. For the preaching of the gospel is nothing else than Christ coming to us, or we being brought to him." — Lathrop

"We are not becoming biblical people in their time and place. Rather, we are becoming more and more our baptized selves." — Ramshaw

"It is then not as history, moral lessons, or beautiful poetry that the scriptures are first of all read. They are read so that the community may encounter the truth about God in Jesus Christ enlivened by the living Spirit. They are read like the passage from Isaiah that Jesus read in the synagogue at Nazareth when he added: "Today this scripture has been fulfilled in your hearing." — Lathrop

"The situation of the one who is reading the Scripture would probably come closest to that in which I read to another person a letter from a friend. I would not read the letter as though I had written it myself. The distance between us would be clearly noticeable as it was read. And yet I would also not be able to read my friend's letter as if it were of no concern to me. On the contrary, because of our close relationship, I would read it with personal interest. Proper reading of Scripture is not a technical exercise that can be learned; it is something that grows or diminishes according to my own spiritual condition. The ponderous, laborious reading of the Bible by many a Christian who has become seasoned through experience often far surpasses a minister's reading, no matter how perfect the latter in form." — Bonhoeffer

✣

Preaching

"Good preaching inevitably leads to situations of pastoral care, just as it also at least partly arises out of paying attention to the needs of life in this place." — Lathrop

"In the final analysis images, paradigms, and models won't do in exercising the office. They talk about the relationship but they don't make it. No doubt the proclamation will include a great deal of such talk about the relationship and that will be necessary, illuminating, and inspiring talk if the preacher is clever and it is done well. But in the final analysis one has to make it. One has to deliver the goods. One has to come out of the woods, move into the present tense, and exercise the office authorized. Here, I say, the possibilities seem to be reduced drastically. One cannot merely play around, publicly, with images. There are a lot of things that don't really help, things which in the final exercise of the office I cannot really say. I can't say, for instance, "I love you," in speaking for God. The "I" gets in the way and confuses the issue. I can only report on the fact that God loves you, or that "God so loved the world that he gave his Son," but then I have slipped out of the first to second person, I to you, discourse into the third person and even into the past tense—God loved the world—and then the office goes begging. You don't even need me to tell you that. You can read all that in the Bible or even in Paul Tillich! The question is what can I say here and now?"—Forde

"Here is an exercise for preachers: Imagine that you have gathered with your entire family at the one-hundredth birthday of your great-grandmother. All the family, all the dozens of descendants of this woman—plus their significant others—are there. It is a great picnic, let us say, in a park. Then, because you are known as a good speaker, you are asked to say something to all that gathering in the park. Your task will be to bring the meaning of this event—something true about your great-grandmother, something true about the party, something true about the identity of the family in the world—to expression in words. The celebration will be marred by phoniness or lying or by talk only about yourself or your experiences. Preaching is like that. Only, in the assembly, it is the church's identity in the merciful Spirit of God and the church's open boundaries in the midst of the world that are being brought to expression."—Lathrop

✜

"In the year 6 Judea was annexed to Syria; in the year 70 Jerusalem and its temple were destroyed. Between these two dates Jesus preached and was crucified on Golgotha. During all that time the life of the little nation was a terrific drama; its patriotic emotions were aroused to the highest pitch and then still more inflamed by the identification of national politics with a national religion. Is it reasonable to assume that what was going on before Jesus' eyes was a closed book, that the agonizing problems of his people were a matter of indifference to him, that he had given them no consideration, that he was not taking a definite attitude towards the great and all-absorbing problem of the very people whom he taught?" — Vladimir Simkhovitch

✜

Response

"All the churches can learn from the widespread African American Christian pattern of support and encouragement and participation with the lone voice of the preacher." — Lathrop

"These two forms of the word — reading and preaching set next to each other and together making up that "word" that is essential — press us beyond, to something more. Lutherans have long responded to the reading and preaching of God's word with the communal singing of the most important hymn of the service, the "hymn of the day." It is as if the single voice of the preacher broadens to become the communal voice of the assembly, all of us, all together, taking up the responsibility of proclamation. Many Christians have further used this place in the service as the place in which the community responds to the word by its confession of faith in the words of one of the classic creeds." — Lathrop

"Under the power of the absolutely unconditional decree — "I love you, you are mine, I will never let you go; you are just for Jesus' sake" — we might begin at least to love God from the heart. When we simply listen to him, that is, we might begin to love him and bear good fruit. Faith born of the unconditional decree, a decree made in spite of everything, will begin to see the truth of the human condition, the reality and totality of human sin in the pursuit of both vices and virtues. Such a faith will begin to see the fantastic magnitude of the divine act, the miracle of a God who nevertheless does business with sinners, and actually begin, however hesitatingly and falteringly, to love God from the heart, to hate sin and the self of sin, and to hope for that righteousness which it knows full well it can never attain by any known scheme of moral or virtuous progress — the righteousness of faith. Such a faith is a death and the beginning of resurrection precisely because it is a belief in the speaking of God which defies all empirical evidence — faith in the promise." — Forde

✣

Abuse of Scripture

"When I was older and was half through college, I chanced to be spending a few days at home near the end of summer vacation. With a feeling of great temerity I asked my grandmother one day why it was that she would not let me read any of the Pauline letters. What she told me I shall never forget. "During the days of slavery," she said, "the master's minister would occasionally hold services for the slaves. Old man McGhee was so mean that he would not let a Negro minister preach to his slaves. Always the white minister used as his text something from Paul. At least three or four times a year he used a text: 'Slaves, be obedient to them that are your masters…, as unto Christ.' Then he would go on to show how it was God's will that we were slaves and how, if we were good and happy slaves, God would bless us. I promised my Maker that if I ever learned to read and if freedom ever came, I would not read that part of the Bible." — Thurman

✤

Proclamation to You!

"Luther's own move is quite simple. He took the 2 Cor. 3:6 passage to mean just what it says: "The letter kills, but the spirit gives life." What the passage describes is an action—not a more or less esoteric method of interpretation. The letter, the written code, kills and through it the spirit gives life. The letter is not something obscure or weak or insufficient. It is not dead because it belongs to the sensible world. Rather, it is deadly, it kills. If the letter has the power to kill, it can by no means be taken lightly, nor can it be circumvented or shunted aside by interpretation. The letter, the whole long history of God's struggle with his people culminating in the cross, spells in the first instance but one thing for the Old Adam. It spells death. The hermeneutic itself is shaped by the death-life language. It takes the shape of the cross: the letter kills the old, and through it, when one at last meets the end of one's sinful ways, the spirit, the life-giving word is given. The scriptures do not provide a mere "jumping-off place" for flights of allegorical and exegetical fancy; they rather cut off such flight. "Spirit" is not some secret inner "level of meaning" that one reaches by intellectual or mystical exercise. The Spirit is precisely the Holy Spirit of God, the Author of the scriptures who uses them as his two-edged sword. The Spirit comes in and through the letter, in and through the concrete history culminating in the cross and resurrection, in and through the proclamation of it to kill and make alive." — Forde

"We are justified freely, for Christ's sake, by faith, without the exertion of our own strength, gaining of merit, or doing of works. To the age old question "What shall I do to be saved?" the confessional answer is shocking: "Nothing! Just be still; shut up and listen for once in your life to what God the Almighty, creator and redeemer, is saying to his world and to you in the death and resurrection of his Son! Listen and believe!" — Forde

"All that we may rightly expect from God, and ask God for, is to be found in Jesus Christ. The God of Jesus Christ has nothing to do with what God, as we imagine God, could do and ought to do." — Bonhoeffer

Reflect: The Creed

The First Article: On Creation

  I believe in God, the Father almighty, creator of heaven and earth.

What does this mean?

  I believe that God has created me together with all that exists. God has given me and still preserves my body and soul: eyes, ears, and all limbs and senses; reason and all mental faculties.

  In addition, God daily and abundantly provides shoes and clothing, food and drink, house and farm, spouse and children, fields, livestock, and all property—along with all the necessities and nourishment for this body and life. God protects me against all danger and shields and preserves me from all evil. And all this is done out of pure, fatherly, and divine goodness and mercy, without any merit or worthiness of mine at all! For all of this I owe it to God to thank and praise, serve and obey him. This is most certainly true.

The Second Article: On Redemption

  I believe in Jesus Christ, God's only Son, our Lord, who was conceived by the Holy Spirit, born of the virgin Mary, suffered under Pontius Pilate, was crucified, died, and was buried; he descended to the dead. On the third day he rose again; he ascended into heaven, he is seated at the right hand of the Father, and he will come to judge the living and the dead.

What does this mean?

    I believe that Jesus Christ, true God, begotten of the Father in eternity, and also a true human being, born of the virgin Mary, is my Lord. He has redeemed me, a lost and condemned human being. He has purchased and freed me from all sins, from death, and from the power of the devil, not with gold or silver, but with his holy, precious blood and with his innocent suffering and death. He has done all this in order that I may belong to him, live under him in his kingdom, and serve him in eternal righteousness, innocence, and blessedness, just as he is risen from the dead and lives and rules eternally. This is most certainly true.

The Third Article: On Being Made Holy

    I believe in the Holy Spirit, the holy catholic church, the communion of saints, the forgiveness of sins, the resurrection of the body, and the life everlasting.

What does this mean?

    I believe that by my own understanding or strength I cannot believe in Jesus Christ my Lord or come to him, but instead the Holy Spirit has called me through the gospel, enlightened me with his gifts, made me holy and kept me in the true faith, just as he calls, gathers, enlightens, and makes holy the whole Christian church on earth and keeps it with Jesus Christ in the one common, true faith. Daily in this Christian church the Holy Spirit abundantly forgives all sins—mine and those of all believers. On the last day the Holy Spirit will raise me and all the dead and will give to me and all believers in Christ eternal life. This is most certainly true.

Question:

What piece of scripture grounds you and won't leave you be? How does it speak to you today?

Pray:

An invitation to prayer:

>Salvation belongs to our God and to Christ the Lamb forever and ever.

Great and wonderful are your deeds, O God of the universe; just and true are your ways, O Ruler of all the nations. Who can fail to honor you, Lord, and sing the glory of your name?

>Salvation belongs to our God and to Christ the Lamb forever and ever.

For you alone are the Holy One, and blessed is the one whose name is the Word of God. All praise and thanks to you, holy God!

>Salvation belongs to our God and to Christ the Lamb forever and ever.

A prayer of Julian of Norwich:

In you, Father all-mighty, we have our preservation and our bliss. In you, Christ, we have our restoring and our saving. You are our mother, brother, and savior. In you, our Lord the Holy Spirit, is marvelous and plenteous grace. You are our clothing; for love you wrap us and embrace us. You are our maker, our lover, our keeper. Teach us to believe that by your grace all shall be well, and all shall be well, and all manner of things shall be well. Amen.

Intercessions:

"Give us today our daily bread."

O God, who gives daily bread without our prayer, even to all evil people, we ask that you would cause us to recognize what our daily bread is—that it includes all things necessary and nourishing for our bodies, from food and shoes to money and good government, good weather and good friends—and cause us to receive it with thanksgiving, through Jesus Christ our Lord. Amen.

✣

Almighty and most merciful God, who has given your word to be the revelation of your great love to humanity, and of your power and will to save us: Grant that our study of it may not be made in vain by the hardness or carelessness of our hearts, but that by it we may be confirmed in penitence, lifted up in hope, made strong for service, and above all, filled with the true knowledge of you and your Son, Jesus Christ. Amen.

✣

That it may please you to give to all people increase of grace to hear and receive your Word, and to bring forth the fruits of the Spirit. Amen.

✣

Everlasting God and Father of our Lord Jesus Christ, grant us thy grace that we may study the Holy Scriptures diligently, and, with our whole heart, seek and find Christ within, and through him obtain everlasting life; through that same Jesus Christ our Lord. Amen.

✣

Continue praying on your own.

Benediction:

Go in peace, share the good news. Amen.

✛

"Worthy is the Lamb that was slain to receive power, and riches, and wisdom, and strength, and honor, and glory, and blessing. Amen." (Rev. 5:12)

THURSDAY

Thursday: Thanksgiving

"Let us lift up our hearts as well as our hands to God in heaven." (Lamentations 3:41)

Read:

Scripture about Thanksgiving:

2 Thessalonians 1:3
Isaiah 6:3
Matthew 21:9
1 Chronicles 16:34

Psalm 34:1
1 Timothy 4:4-5
Psalm 148

Scripture from Jesus' death:

Luke 22:1-6
Mark 14:12-25
John 13:1-17
Matthew 26:36-46

Luke 22:54-62
Matthew 27:32-44
Mark 15:33-41
John 19:38-42

Meditations to Reflect upon:

The Community in Prayer

"The presider is inviting others in the practice of the prayer: "Let *us* pray," she or he calls out. In spite of our widespread North American cultural experience, the prayer is not an individual exercise, "give *us*, forgive *us*, save *us*," we say in the archetypal prayer, and that communal meaning must be learned again by heart, in the first case by the presider." — Lathrop

"Every Christian is invited to pray. The Christian community has classically understood itself as a priesthood standing together before God, interceding for the needs of the world. Furthermore, the rhythm of Sunday assembly, marking the week with the resurrection gospel and with its thanksgivings and its intercessions, has flowed out into the life of the week with an answering rhythm of daily prayer, morning and evening, whereby at least some Christians mark the cardinal points of the day with signs of the gospel, with the praise of God, and with prayers for the life of the world. Even when a Christian participates very modestly in that rhythm — a few prayers at table, a Lord's Prayer at bedtime, an urgent prayer at a time of the neighbor's illness or a friend's death — she or he still stands before God as a member of the priesthood. She or he still claims and lives from that astonishing, over-the-top promise of the Jesus of the Gospels, "Ask, and it will be given you." Christian prayer may thus be a quite personal matter, but it is never alone, never individualist. Christians pray with Jesus Christ, in the power of the Spirit. They thus pray with those who are "in Christ," with those whom the Spirit enlivens and in whom the Spirit groans. They pray with the church." — Lathrop

"And on the day named after the sun all, whether they lived in the city or the countryside, are gathered together in unity. Then the records of the apostles or the writings of the prophets are read for as long as there is time. When the reader has concluded, the presider in a discourse admonishes and invites us into the pattern of these good things. Then we all stand together and offer prayer." — Justin Martyr

✣

"In intercessory prayer the face that may have been strange and intolerable to me is transformed into the face of one for whom Christ died, the face of a pardoned sinner." — Bonhoeffer

✣

Thanksgiving

"This cross is the tree of my eternal salvation nourishing and delighting me. I take root in its roots, I am extended in its branches. In my tent I am shaded by its shade. Its flowers are my flowers; I am wholly delighted by its fruits. This cross is my nourishment when I am hungry, my fountain when I am thirsty, my covering when I am stripped, for my leaves are no longer fig leaves but the breath of life. This is the ladder of Jacob, the way of angels. This is my tree, wide as the firmament, which extends from earth to the heavens. It is the pillar of the universe, the support of the whole world." — The Pasch History

"Martin Luther reminds us never to claim too much

for the church's worship. Our faith, instead, is that God will save the world." — Ramshaw

"Anne Lamott says, "Thank you, Thank you, Thank you" and "Help me, Help me, Help me" are also profound prayers, or in our terms, prayers within the deepest language of the praying community, prayers with the church." — Lathrop

✠

"Blessed is God who cares for the salvation of souls." — Father Zossima

✠

Thank God!

"Suppose there is a lowly peasant lad who has a secret love for a beautiful princess. It seems a hopeless, lost love. He fears he can't have her so he only worships from afar. In his hurt he takes steps to defend himself. He constructs a kind of defense mechanism, a kind of "fictional theology" about her if you will. He tells himself that she is too vain and proud for her own good. She consorts with all the wrong people — with princes, not with peasant lads. Yet he dreams that maybe he can make it somehow. He sets out to show her. He sets out to become rich and powerful. He plans and plots and sets ideals for himself. He dreams of himself as a potential prince! But then to top it all off he hears that she has already been predestined for someone. She has already decided the matter. That, of course, would be the last, crushing blow. But he refuses to believe it and goes on doggedly pursuing his ideals and perhaps even begins to become cruel and ruthless in his frustration and anger.

Then suppose one fine day the royal carriage comes clattering down the road and pulls up at the door. The princess steps down and comes to him and announces, "John, what in the world are you up to? Don't you see? You are the one I have decided on! I love you and always have. Why are you making such a fool of yourself?"

"Who me? Holy Smokes!" — Forde

"When you sing 'Come into my heart, Lord Jesus,' be assured. He will come. But he will bring with him — into your heart and into your life — all those who belong to him: all the little ones; all the wretched; all the poor. If you pray alone in your closet, it will suddenly be full." — Lathrop

"I have long found deep comfort in the words that Martin Luther wrote on a note found by his bedside when he himself was found dead in 1546. As recorded in the famous Table Talk, his deathbed note included this little assertion: "I say we are all beggars; this is true." Having learned about "growing in grace" and "sanctification" when I was a boy, studying my catechism, I often wondered if I was really making any progress. I thought probably not. But Luther helped me to see that growth in grace might really mean growing in need, growing in identification with a needy world and with other needy folk, growth in becoming more and more profoundly a beggar oneself, waiting upon God." — Lathrop

"We know that God and the devil are locked together in combat over the world and that the devil has a word to say even at death. In the face of death we cannot say in a fatalistic way, "It is God's will"; we must add the opposite: "It is not God's will." Death shows that the world is not what it should be, but that it needs redemption.

Christ alone overcomes death. Here, "It is God's will" and "It is not God's will" come to the most acute paradox and balance each other out. God agrees to be involved in something that is not the divine will, and from now on death must serve God despite itself. From now on, "It is God's will" also embraces "It is not God's will." God's will is the overcoming of death through the death of Jesus Christ. Only in the cross and resurrection of Jesus Christ has death come under God's power, must it serve the purpose of God. Not a fatalistic surrender, but living faith in Jesus Christ, who died and has risen again for us, can seriously make an end of death for us." — Bonhoeffer

✛

"Robert Jenson puts it in a recent study on the Confessional writings, our lives in this age are shaped by conditional promises and statements. Conditional promises are "if-then" promises. If you fulfill the required conditions then the promise will be fulfilled. "If you eat your spinach…,then you will get your dessert." If you put the coin in the slot, then you will get the candy bar. If you study hard, then you will get good grades and maybe a scholarship to Yale or Harvard. If you do your job well, then you will get a promotion or a raise, or get called to a big city congregation or be made a bishop or a full professor. Always 'if-then." Almost everything we live with is conditional and so it must be here.

The gospel of justification by faith is such a shocker, such an explosion, because it is an absolutely unconditional promise. It is not an "if-then" kind of statement, but a "because-therefore" pronouncement: Because Jesus died and rose, your sins are forgiven and you are righteous in the sight of God! It bursts in upon our little world all shut up and barricaded behind our accustomed conditional thinking as some strange comet from goodness knows where, something we can't really seem to wrap our minds around, the logic of which appears closed to us. How can it be entirely unconditional? Isn't it terribly dangerous? How can anyone say flat-out, "You are righteous for Jesus' sake? Is there not some price to be paid, some-thing (however miniscule) to be done? After all, there can't be such a thing as a free lunch, can there?" —Forde

✣

"Nothing can make up for the absence of someone whom we love, and it would be wrong to try to find a substitute; we must simply hold out and see it through. That sounds very hard at first, but at the same time it is a great consolation, for the gap, as long as it remains unfilled, preserves the bonds between us. It is nonsense to say that God fills the gap; God does not fill it, but on the contrary, God keeps it empty and so helps us keep alive our former communion with each other, even at the cost of pain." —Bonhoeffer

Reflect: The Lord's Prayer

Introduction:

Our Father in heaven.

What does this mean?

With these words God wants to attract us, so that we come to believe he is truly our Father and we are truly his children, in order that we may ask him boldly and with complete confidence, just as loving children ask their father.

The First Petition:

Hallowed be your name.

What does this mean?

It is true that God's name is holy in itself, but we ask in this prayer that it may also become holy in and among us.

How does this come about?

Whenever the word of God is taught clearly and purely and we, as God's children, also live holy lives according to it. To this end help us, dear Father in heaven! However, whoever teaches and lives otherwise than the word of God teaches, dishonors the name of God among us. Preserve us from this, heavenly Father!

Second Petition:

Your Kingdom Come.

What does this mean?

In fact, God's kingdom comes on its own without our prayer, but we ask in this prayer that it may also come to us.

How does this come about?

Whenever our heavenly Father gives us his Holy Spirit, so that through the Holy Spirit's grace we believe God's holy word and live godly lives here in time and hereafter in eternity.

The Third Petition:

Your will be done, on earth as in heaven.

What does this mean?

In fact, God's good and gracious will comes about without our prayer, but we ask in this prayer that it may also come about in and among us.

How does this come about?

Whenever God breaks and hinders every evil scheme and will — as are present in the will of the devil, the word, and our flesh — that would not allow us to hallow God's name and would prevent the coming of his kingdom, and instead whenever God strengthens us and keeps us steadfast in his word and in faith until the end of our lives. This is God's gracious and good will.

The Fourth Petition:

Give us today our daily bread.

What does this mean?

In fact, God gives daily bread without our prayer, even to all evil people, but we ask in this prayer that God cause us to recognize what our daily bread is and to receive it with thanksgiving.

What then does "daily bread" mean?

Everything included in the necessities and nourishment for our bodies, such as food, drink, clothing, shoes, house, farm, fields, livestock, money, property, an upright spouse, upright children, upright members of the household, upright and faithful rulers, good government, good weather, peace, health, decency, honor, good friends, faithful neighbors, and the like.

The Fifth Petition:

Forgive us our sins, as we forgive those who sin against us.

What does this mean?

We ask in this prayer that our heavenly Father would not regard our sins nor deny these petitions on their account, for we are worthy of nothing for which we ask, nor have we earned it. Instead, we ask that God would give us all things by grace, for we daily sin much and indeed deserve only punishment. So, on the other hand, we, too, truly want to forgive heartily and to do good gladly to those who sin against us.

The Sixth Petition:

Save us from the time of trial.

What does this mean?

It is true that God tempts no one, but we ask in this prayer that God would preserve and keep us, so that the devil, the world, and our flesh may not deceive us or mislead us into false belief, despair, and other great and shameful sins, and that, although we may be attacked by them, we may finally prevail and gain the victory.

The Seventh Petition:

And deliver us from evil.

What does this mean?

We ask in this prayer, as in a summary, that our Father in heaven may deliver us from all kinds of evil—affecting body or soul, property or reputation—and at the last, when our final hour comes, may grant us a blessed end and take us by grace from this valley of tears to himself in heaven.

Conclusion:

For the kingdom, the power, and the glory are yours, now and forever. Amen

What does this mean?

That I should be certain that such petitions are acceptable to, and heard by, our Father in heaven, for he himself commanded us to pray like this and has promised to hear us. "Amen, amen" means "Yes, yes, it is going to come about just like this."

Question:

What are you most thankful for? Remember to thank God for this in your prayers.

Try shortening the Lord's Prayer up in light of Luther's explanations in order to let it's meaning fall fresh upon your soul.

For example, I got it down to 8 words, "I bow in trust, forgive, save, sustain, here."

Pray:

An invitation to prayer:

Holy, Holy, Holy Lord, God of power and might, heaven and earth are full of your glory.

Hosanna in the highest. Blessed is he who comes in the name of the Lord. Hosanna in the highest. Hosanna in the highest.

A prayer of Martin Luther:

Behold, Lord, an empty vessel that needs to be filled. My Lord, fill it. I am weak in the faith; strengthen me. I am cold in love; warm me and make me fervent, that my love may go out to my neighbor. I do not have a strong and firm faith; at times I doubt and am unable to trust you altogether. O Lord, help me. Strengthen my faith and trust in you. In you I have sealed the treasure of all I have. I am poor; you are rich and came to be merciful to the poor. I am a sinner; you are upright. With me, there is an abundance of sin; in you is the fullness of righteousness. Therefore I will remain with you, of whom I can receive, but to whom I may not give. Amen.

Intercessions:

"Forgive us our sins, as we forgive those who sin against

us."

We pray Heavenly Father, that you would not regard our sins nor deny our petitions on account of our sins. For we are worthy of nothing for which we ask, nor have we earned it.

Please give to us all things by grace, for we daily sin and indeed deserve only punishment.

Help us, for our part, to heartily forgive and gladly do good for those who have sinned against us. We pray this through Jesus Christ our Lord. Amen.

✜

Almighty God, Father of all mercies, we humbly thank you for your goodness to us and to all that you have made.

We praise you for your creation, for keeping us and all things in your care, and for all the blessings of life.

Above all we bless you for your immeasurable love in redeeming the world by our Lord Jesus Christ, for the means of grace, and for the hope of glory.

And, we pray, give us such an awareness of your mercies that with thankful hearts we praise you, not only with our lips but in our lives, by giving ourselves to your service and by living in your gifts of holiness and righteousness all our days; through Jesus Christ our Lord, to whom, with you and the Holy Spirit, be all worship and praise, now and forever. Amen.

✜

Thank you for the beauty and wonder of your creation, in earth and sky and sea.

Thank you for all that is gracious in the lives of men and women, revealing the image of Christ.

Thank you for our daily food and drink, our homes and families, and for our friends.

Thank you for minds to think, and hearts to love, and hands to serve.

Thank you for health and strength to work, and leisure to rest and play.

Thank you for the brave and courageous, who are patient in suffering and faithful in adversity.

Thank you for all valiant seekers after truth, liberty, and justice.

Thank you for the communion of saints in all times and places.

Above all we give you thanks for the great mercies and promises given to us in Christ Jesus our Lord.

Amen.

✣

Continue praying on your own.

Benediction:

"Now unto him that is able to keep us from falling, and to present us faultless before the presence of his glory with exceeding joy, to the only wise God our Savior, be glory and majesty, dominion and power, both now and ever. Amen." (Jude 24-25)

✣

Go in peace. Serve the Lord. Amen.

FRIDAY

Friday: The Meal

"For I received from the Lord what I also handed on to you, that the Lord Jesus on the night when he was betrayed took a loaf of bread, and when he had given thanks, he broke it and said, "This is my body that is for you. Do this in remembrance of me." In the same way he took the cup also, after supper, saying, "This cup is the new covenant in my blood. Do this, as often as you drink it, in remembrance of me." For as often as you eat this bread and drink this cup, you proclaim the Lord's death until he comes."

(1 Corinthians 11:23-26)

Read:

Scripture about The Meal:

Luke 22:19-20	Luke 24:28-31
Acts 2:42	Isaiah 6:3
John 6:51	Matthew 21:9
Exodus 12:1-51	

Scripture from Jesus' Resurrection:

Mark 16:1-8	John 20:24-29
Luke 24:13-35	Acts 1:6-11
Matthew 28:16-20	

Meditations to Reflect upon

Eating Together

"Quite concretely, quite physically, Christianity is a meeting. Or, more exactly, the Christianity that is associated with the four Gospels is a specific kind of meeting: it is a meal fellowship. As such, this Christianity is an invitation for us together to see both God and the world anew from the perspective of that table, or that shared food." — Lathrop

"In my own experience in a small, rural parish in southern Idaho, I would often marvel at the spiritual mothers, that is, the older women who listened to the cares and troubles of younger men and women struggling in their marriages, who chose to serve as "godmothers of prayer" for the junior high religion students, and never tired of providing food and support for families whose loved ones were ill or had died." — Forman

"Justin concluded his defense of the faith with a hugely important meal account. Christians remind each other that they are baptized, he wrote to the emperor Antonius Pius, by repeatedly meeting together, by giving thanks over what they eat, and by sharing that food with the hungry and the poor." — Lathrop

"Several further things should be noted about this important description. The meal was held every Sunday, immediately following the scripture reading, preaching, and prayers. The presider gave thanks — as well or as long as he or she could — but everyone participated in this thanksgiving, both by their audible amen and by their eating and drinking. The loaf and the cup of communion were sent to those who could not be with the assembly—whether because of sickness or imprisonment or their status as slaves is not clear—by the hands of table-servers or deacons. A collection was always made for the poor. Such a collection of food and money belongs essentially to the Christian meal and is one source of our continued practice of taking a collection on Sunday." — Lathrop

✣

A Dangerous Meal

"Especially at Communion times he is in a great confusion, as being not only to receive God, but to break, and administer him. Neither finds he any issue in this, but to throw himself down at the throne of grace." — The Parson in Sacraments

"I found myself much warned by a saying attributed to Chrysostom: "The road to hell is paved with priest's skulls." And I found myself much comforted by a saying attributed to Augustine: "Insofar as I am a bishop [read, presider] I am in danger; insofar as I am a believer [read, member of the assembly; baptized Christian] I am safe." — Lathrop

✣

Meeting Christ

"When, in 1519 Martin Luther wrote of the practice of the mass, he urged communicants to understand that meal as an amazing exchange, the very "commerce" of the city of God. In the Holy Communion, Christ and all of his holy ones take our wretchedness and, in exchange, give us their blessedness. In turn, we are to direct ourselves toward our neighbors in need, continuing the exchange, God does not need what we have to give. Our neighbors do. He continued: " When you have partaken of this sacrament, therefore, or desire to partake of it, you must in turn share the misfortunes of the fellowship, as has been said...here your heart must go out in love and learn that this is a sacrament of love. As love and support are given to you, you in turn must render love and support to Christ in his needy ones. You must feel with sorrow all the dishonor done to Christ in his holy Word, all the misery of Christendom, all the unjust suffering of the innocent, with which the world is everywhere filled to overflowing. You must fight, work, pray, and — if you cannot do more — have heartfelt sympathy." — Lathrop

"Christians have believed that baptism itself is immersion in the very river of the water of life and that to eat of the holy communion is to eat from the tree of life. These images of the magnificent, life-giving tree and the all-refreshing river are, of course, used in the Revelation as metaphors for the presence and grace of God in Jesus Christ. Word and sacrament apply that grace to human lives like the healing leaves, the reviving water, the life-giving fruit." — Lathrop

"Christian faith is more than an idea and more than the centrality of our own choice. Say it this way: Christian worship is the communal encounter with the grace of God incarnate in Jesus Christ, and it involves the encounter with those concrete, flesh-and-blood things that connect us to the flesh of Jesus and so engage us in that grace." — Lathrop

✜

The Physicality of It

"We are all far more aware than we used to be about the power of actions to form values and shape minds. The education of children is achieved not only by years of reading and hours of storytelling. Rather, by attending interactive museums, creating art, building models, participating in pageants and other such activities, children plant their learning into their psyches more firmly than they would by listening to someone else talk. If we hope to rear our children as Christians, we cannot only talk to them of Christ. We need to find ways for them to join us to enact the meaning of Christ." — Ramshaw

"These things also connect us to the concrete, real earth. Even though we may say that we have these things simply because they are what actually come to us from the culture in which Jesus was born and from the church's history, Christian faith has believed that the universal availability of the stuff of these central symbols has been and is a gift from God. Water is everywhere. Humans need it simply to live. Baptism is in water, any water, local water, not some special or Near Eastern water. Understandable but strongly symbolic speech, used to convey the deepest human values or pray the longings of the human heart, is found in every culture. The oral witness to Jesus Christ can be made in it, speaking out the needs of all the earth. Festive meals are found universally. The Lord's supper is held with local bread and local wine — or, where these are simply not available or are far too expensive or too alien with locally recognized staple food and festive drink — not with special, imported food. The things in which we encounter Jesus Christ, and in him God's overflowing grace for all, are accessible everywhere.

They are signs of the goodness of God's earth, as well as signs for the deep unity God's mercy can establish between the good diversity of the many cultures of the world." — Lathrop

Reflect: The Sacrament of the Altar

What is the Sacrament of the Altar?

It is the true body and blood of our Lord Jesus Christ under the bread and wine, instituted by Christ himself for us Christians to eat and to drink.

Where is this written?

The holy evangelists Matthew, Mark, and Luke — and St. Paul, writes thus:

"In the night in which he was betrayed, our Lord Jesus took bread, and gave thanks; broke it, and gave it for his disciples, saying: Take and eat; this is my body, given for you. Do this for the remembrance of me. Again, after supper, he took the cup, gave thanks, and gave it for all to drink, saying: This cup is the new covenant in my blood, shed for you and for all people for the forgiveness of sin. Do this for the remembrance of me."

What is the benefit of such eating and drinking?

The words "given for you" and "shed for you for the forgiveness of sin" show us that forgiveness of sin, life, and salvation are given to us in the sacrament through these words, because where there is forgiveness of sin, there is also life and salvation.

How can bodily eating and drinking do such a great thing?

Eating and drinking certainly do not do it, but rather the words that are recorded: "given for you" and "shed for you for the forgiveness of sin." These words, when accompanied by the physical eating and drinking, are the essential thing in the sacrament, and whoever believes these very words has what they declare and state, namely, "forgiveness of sin."

Who, then, receives this sacrament worthily?

Fasting and bodily preparation are in fact a fine external discipline, but a person who has faith in these words, "given for you" and "shed for you for the forgiveness of sin," is really worthy and well prepared. However, a person who does no believe these words or doubts them is unworthy and unprepared, because the words "for you" require truly believing hearts.

Question:

When we consume something it becomes part of us. How has the body of Christ been part of you this week? How have you been a part of the body of Christ?

Pray:

An invitation to prayer:

Lamb of God, you take away the sin of the world; have mercy on us.

Lamb of God, you take away the sin of the world; have mercy upon us.

Lamb of God, you take away the sin of the world; grant us peace.

A prayer of Mother Teresa of Calcutta:

Make us worthy, Lord, to serve our fellow human beings throughout the world who live and die in poverty and hunger. Give them through our hands this day their daily bread, and by our understanding love, give peace and joy. Amen.

Intercessions:

"Save us from the time of trial."

O God, who tempts no one, we pray please preserve and keep us, so that the devil, the world, and our flesh may not deceive or mislead us into false belief, despair, and other great and shameful sins, and that, although we may be so attacked by them, we may finally prevail and gain the victory, through Jesus Christ, your Son, our Lord. Amen.

✣

God our Father, whose Son our Lord Jesus Christ in a wonderful sacrament has left us a memorial of his passion: Grant us so to venerate the sacred mysteries of his

Body and Blood, that we may ever perceive within ourselves the fruit of his redemption; who lives and reigns with you and the Holy Spirit, one God forever and ever. Amen.

✜

O Lord Jesus Christ, you daily give us our earthly bread, grant, we pray, that we may know that you are eager to give us more than bread. You invite us to your table; make us willing to come and eat, that we may be filled with all the fullness of your grace; for your name's sake. Amen.

✜

Feed we pray, all those who hunger, all those who go without. Make us ever more conscious of their presence that we might be among them — as your Son reminded us we are. Grant that whether I am fasting or feasting my body's desire might be for your table, where none go hungry, but all find bread that satisfies. Amen.

✜

Continue praying on your own.

Benediction:

"The God of all hope fill us with all joy and peace in believing, that we may abound in hope, in the power of the Holy Spirit. Amen (Rom 15:13)

✜

May the blessing of the eternal God be upon us, and upon our work and worship: His light to guide us, His presence to strengthen us, His love to unite us; Now and always. Amen.

SATURDAY

Saturday: The Sending

"As the Father has sent me, so I send you." (John 20:21)

Read:

Scripture about the Sending:

Matthew 28:19-20
Numbers 6:23-26
Romans 12:11
Matthew 10:7

Galatians 2:10
Psalm 96:3
Acts 1:8

Scripture from the Christian Letters:

Romans 8:18-39
Romans 13:8-10
1 Corinthians 1:18-25
Galatians 3:27-29
Galatians 5:22-26

Philippians 2:5-11
1 Peter 3:18-22
1 John 4:7-12
Revelation 5:4-6

Meditations to Reflect upon

"The people who love, because they are freed through the truth of God, are the most revolutionary people on earth." — Bonhoeffer

✤

The Neighbor

"The Religion of Jesus makes the love-ethic central. This is no ordinary achievement. It seems clear that Jesus started out with the simple teaching concerning love embodied in the timeless words of Israel: "Hear, O Israel: The Lord our God is one Lord: and thou shall love the Lord thy God with all thy heart, and with all thy soul, and with all thy might," and "thy neighbour as thyself." Once the neighbor is defined, then one's moral obligation is clear. In a memorable story Jesus defined the neighbor by telling of the Good Samaritan. With sure artistry and great power he depicted what happens when a man responds directly to human need across the barriers of class, race, and condition. Every man is potentially every other man's neighbor. Neighborliness is nonspatial; it is qualitative. A man must love his neighbor directly, clearly, permitting no barriers between." — Thurman

"Jesus stands at the door and knocks, in complete reality. He asks you for help in the form of a beggar, in the form of a ruined human being in torn clothing. He confronts you in every person that you meet. Christ walks on the earth as your neighbor as long as there are people." — Bonhoeffer

"If we want to understand God's goodness in God's gifts, then we must think of them as a responsibility we bear for our brothers and sisters." — Bonhoeffer

"Wherever Christians are, justification by grace through faith calls them to speak and to work for reconciliation, justice, love, peace, and truth; to hear confession and to speak forgiveness; and to give caring service attentive to the neighbors' needs." — Krych

"Once one has been cured of all heaven-storming ambitions one suddenly finds God's creation to care about and for." — Forde

"Theodora teaches that the virtues of true midwives of people's spiritual lives are patience, gentleness, and humility — the complete opposites to domination, vainglory, and pride." — Forman

✤

The Dangers of Being Sent

"This impulse at the heart of Christianity is the human will to share with others what one has found meaningful to oneself elevated to the height of a moral imperative. But there is a lurking danger in this very emphasis. It is exceedingly difficult to hold oneself free from a certain contempt for those whose predicament makes moral appeal for defense and succor." — Thurman

"It has long been a matter of serious moment that for decades we have studied the various people of the world and those who live as our neighbors as objects of missionary endeavor and enterprise without being at all willing to treat them either as brothers or as human beings. I say this without rancor, because it is not an issue in which vicious human beings are involved. But it is one of the subtle perils of a religion which calls attention—to the point of overemphasis, sometimes—to one's obligation to administer to human need." —Thurman

✛

"Perpetuating injustice does harm. Indeed, the evil one wants to accomplish only one thing with you; namely, that you also become evil. But were that to happen, the evil one would have won. Therefore, repay no one evil for evil. For in so doing, you harm not the evil one but yourself." —Bonhoeffer

✛

"Classic Christian fasting is conjoined with intercessory prayer for a world in need and with almsgiving—with the sharing of the food and money we are not consuming ourselves—as a sign of the solidarity of our life with those whose lives of poverty are their only prayer. One of the Prayers of the Day appointed for Ash Wednesday reads as follows: "Merciful God, accompany our journey through these forty days. Renew us by our baptism to provide for those who are poor, to pray for those in need, and to fast from self-indulgence, that we may find our treasure in the life of your Son, Jesus Christ, our Savior and Lord." —Lathrop

✛

The Body of Christ

"We ourselves have been made again into what we eat: body of Christ for our neighbors. So we then leave, on mission to live out our hope amid the conditions of the world, to turn toward others beyond this circle, to (like Jeremiah) "buy the field" in the circumstances of our life, to act out some of the justice for which we have prayed, to share food as it has been shared here, to honor the earth like the gifts of the earth have been welcomed respectfully and solidarity that have been shown to us. "Go in peace. Serve the Lord," cries out one of the lay ministers assisting the assembly. Or, more recently, to make the service of the Lord more explicit and to recall, with Paul, the one challenge made by the first church council ever held, the lay assisting minister says, "Go in peace. Remember the poor." "Thanks be to God," we say and go." — Lathrop

"In the body of Christ all humanity is accepted, included, and borne, and that the church-community of believers is to make this known to the world by word and life. This means not being separated from the world, but calling the world into the community of the body of Christ…The church-community is separated from the world only by this: it believes in the reality of being accepted by God — a reality that belongs to the whole world — and in affirming this as valid for itself it witnesses that it is valid for the entire world." — Bonhoeffer

"Christ took upon himself this human form of ours. He became human even as we are women and men. In his humanity and his lowliness we recognize our own form. He has become like a man, so that people should be like him. And in the Incarnation the whole human race recovers the dignity of the image of God. Henceforth, any attack even on the least of people is an attack on Christ." — Bonhoeffer

✠

The Church in the World

"The Church exists by missions, just as a fire exists by burning." —Emil Brunner

"Open yourself to all that is human and you will find that every vain desire to escape from the world disappears. Be present to your age; adapt yourself to the conditions of the moment. Father, I pray you not to take them out of the world, but to keep them from evil." —Frère Roger

"We cannot be honest unless we recognize that we have to live in the world *etsi dues non daretur*. And this is just what we do recognize—before God! God himself compels us to recognize it. So our coming of age leads us to a true recognition of our situation before God. God would have us know that we must live as people who manage our lives without God. The God who is with us is the God who forsakes us. The God who lets us live in the world without the working hypothesis of God is the God before whom we stand continually. Before God and with God we live without God. God lets the divine self be pushed out of the world onto the cross. God is weak and powerless in the world, and that is precisely the way, the only way, in which God is with us and helps us. Matthew 8:17 makes it quite clear that Christ helps us, not by virtue of his omnipotence, but by virtue of his weakness and suffering." —Bonhoeffer

"make the world our parish, not our parish the world." —John Wesley

✠

"Good works should be quite as natural and spontaneous as a parent running to pick up and comfort a child who has fallen and gotten hurt. One doesn't stop to think about it ("Let me see now, should I do this or shouldn't I? Is it necessary?"); one doesn't even worry about whether it is a good work or not—one just does it. And after it is over, one forgets about it completely. That is what good works are like. They are probably those works we have forgotten all about." —Forde

Reflect: The 4th through 10th commandments

The Fourth Commandment:

    Honor your father and your mother.

What does this mean?

    We are to fear and love God, so that we neither despise nor anger our parents and others in authority, but instead honor, serve, obey, love, and respect them.

The Fifth Commandment:

    You shall not murder.

What does this mean?

    We are to fear and love God, so that we neither endanger nor harm the lives of our neighbors, but instead help and support them in all of life's needs.

The Sixth Commandment:

    You shall not commit adultery.

What does this mean?

    We are to fear and love God, so that we lead pure and decent lives in word and deed, and each of us loves and honors his or her spouse.

The Seventh Commandment:

    You shall not steal.

What does this mean?

> We are to fear and love God, so that we neither take our neighbors' money or property, nor acquire them by using shoddy merchandise or crooked deals, but instead help them to improve and protect their property and income.

The Eighth Commandment:

> You shall not bear false witness against your neighbor.

What does this mean?

> We are to fear and love God, so that we do not tell lies about our neighbors, betray or slander them, or destroy their reputations. Instead we are to come to their defense, speak well of them, and interpret everything they do in the best possible light.

The Ninth Commandment:

> You shall not covet your neighbor's house.

What does this mean?

> We are to fear and love God, so that we do not try to trick our neighbors out of their inheritance or property or try to get it for ourselves by claiming to have a legal right to it and the like, but instead be of help and service to them in keeping what is theirs.

The Tenth Commandment:

You shall not covet your neighbor's wife, or male or female slave, or ox, or donkey, or anything that belongs to your neighbor.

What does this mean?

We are to fear and love God, so that we do not entice, force, or steal away from our neighbors their spouses, household workers, or livestock, but instead urge them to stay and fulfill their responsibilities to our neighbors.

What then does God say about all these commandments?

God says the following: "I, the Lord your God, am a jealous God, punishing children for the iniquity of parents, to the third and the fourth generation of those who reject me, but showing steadfast love to the thousandth generation of those who love me and keep my commandants."

What does this mean?

God threatens to punish all who break these commandments. Therefore, we are to fear his wrath and not disobey these commandments. However, God promises grace and every good thing to all those who keep these commandments. Therefore we also are to love and trust him and gladly act according to his commands.

Question:

How are you doing living the Christian faith outside the church walls? To where are you being called?

Pray:

An invitation to prayer:

Now Lord, you let your servant go in peace: your word has been fulfilled.

My own eyes have seen the salvation, which you have prepared in the sight of every people: a light to reveal you to the nations and the glory of your people Israel.

Now Lord, let your servant go in peace.

A Prayer of St. Patrick:

Christ with me, Christ before me, Christ behind me,

Christ in me, Christ beneath me, Christ above me,

Christ on my right, Christ on my left,

Christ when I lie down, Christ when I sit down, Christ when I arise,

Christ in the heart of every person who thinks of me,

Christ in the mouth of everyone who speak of me,

Christ in every eye that sees me,

Christ in every ear that hears me.

Intercessions:

"And deliver us from evil."

Our Father in heaven, deliver us from all kinds of evil, whether they affect body or soul, property or reputation—and at last, when our final hour comes, grant us a blessed end and take us by grace from this valley of tears to yourself, through Jesus Christ, your Son, our Lord. Amen.

✦

Keep watch, dear Lord, with those who work or watch or weep, and give your angels charge over those who sleep. Tend the sick, give rest to the weary, bless the dying, soothe the suffering, comfort the afflicted, shield the joyous; and all for your love's sake. Amen.

✦

Almighty God, our Heavenly Father, who declares your glory and shows forth your handiworks in the heavens and in the earth: Deliver us, we ask, in our several callings, from the service of mammon, that we may do the work which You give to us in truth, in beauty, and in righteousness, with singleness of heart as your servants, and to the benefit of our fellows; for the sake of him who came among us as one that served, your Son, Jesus Christ, our Lord. Amen.

✦

O God, give us grace to set a good example to all among whom we live, to be just and true in all our dealings, to be strict and conscientious in the discharge of every duty; pure and temperate in all enjoyment, gracious and generous and courteous toward all; so that the mind of Christ Jesus may be formed in us and all may know that we are his disciples; in whose name we pray. Amen.

✣

Continue praying on your own.

Benediction:

"the peace of God, which surpasses all understanding, will guard your hearts and your minds in Christ Jesus." (Philippians 4:7)

✣

Almighty God, by the power of the Spirit you have knit your servants into the one body of your Son, Jesus Christ. Give us courage, patience, and vision; and strengthen us all in our Christian vocation of witness to the world and of service to others; through Jesus Christ our Lord.

Amen.

The Evening Blessing:

In the evening, when you go to bed, you are to make the sign of the holy cross and say:

"God the Father, Son, and Holy Spirit watch over me. Amen."

Then, kneeling or standing, say the Apostle's Creed and the Lord's Prayer. If you wish, you may in addition recite this little prayer as well:

"I give thanks to you, heavenly Father, through Jesus Christ your dear son, that you have graciously protected me today. I ask you to forgive me all my sins, where I have done wrong, and graciously to protect me tonight. Into your hands I commend myself, my body, my soul, and all that is mine. Let your holy angels be with me, so that the wicked foe may have no power over me. Amen."

Then you are to go to sleep quickly and cheerfully.

Made in the USA
Middletown, DE
26 December 2014